Title: Unleashing Your Sales Potential : Maximizing Profits with Proven Sales Techniques.

Richard T. Trojan

Introduction

why you need to unleashing your sale potential

Freedom

Take control of your advanced sales program learning experience with the Executive Program's flexible online approach. Adopting this novel technique allows you to learn at your own speed, without regard for time or place. No matter where you are in the world, you can build your own path to success without jeopardizing your current professional obligations. Whether you're a seasoned expert trying to enhance your skill set or an aspiring sales professional searching for advanced certification, the online format offers unprecedented ease and accessibility, tailored to your busy schedule.

Learn from Sales Industry Titans

Prepare to be coached by sales specialists and industry leaders who have mastered the sales war. These mentors give you vital insights and best practices that have molded their remarkable careers, drawing on their wealth of experience and unique expertise. You'll develop a strategic mentality and acquire the tools needed to overcome real-world sales issues with their guidance. Prepare to emerge as a force of nature, armed with the knowledge and confidence to leave your imprint on the sales business.

How to Master the Art of Future-Ready Sales

Adaptability is critical as technology continues to reshape the sales landscape. The Executive Program prepares you for the future by including lessons on using technology for sales, delving into the intricacies of data analytics, and harnessing the untamed power of social media. Developing an advanced sales program that is digitally savvy Strategist positions you as a valuable asset to any firm, capable of navigating the industry's ever-changing currents.

The Conclusion: A New Chapter in Sales Excellence

Investing in the Executive Program in Strategic Sales Management opens the door to a revolutionary and influential sales career. You position yourself as a high-performing and dynamic Sales Strategist by gaining skills in strategic sales management, employing digital tools, and learning from industry trailblazers. Accept this exceptional opportunity to become future-ready in the sales area and open new doors to personal and professional development.

CHAPTER 1

Mastering Communication

Welcome to a thrilling adventure in the world of sales! Whether you're a seasoned expert trying to sharpen your skills or a beginner eager to succeed, this article will provide you with the necessary knowledge and tactics for sales success.

1. Recognizing the Key Selling Points:

A firm foundation is required for effective salesmanship. Here are three important aspects to remember:

a) Establish Meaningful Connections: Sales is about more than just selling business; it's about making meaningful connections. Take the time to learn about your clients' wants and problem spots. Active listening, empathy, and individualized interactions can help you build trust and rapport.

b) Product Knowledge: In order to market a product or service, you must first understand it thoroughly. Spend time researching your offerings, keeping up with industry changes, and establishing expertise. This expertise will increase your confidence and trustworthiness, allowing you to properly resolve consumer concerns.

d) Effective Communication: Effective communication skills are essential in sales. Develop your abilities to explain value propositions, respond to objections, and tailor your pitch to specific clients. To engage your audience and make a lasting impact, master the art of storytelling.

2. Becoming the Office's Best Salesperson:
Consider the following techniques to distinguish yourself as a top performer in your office:

a) Ongoing Learning: Sales is an ever-changing field. Maintain your curiosity and commitment to learning. To broaden your expertise, attend workshops, seminars, and industry events. Self-study can be accomplished through the use of books, podcasts, and online resources. The more you understand, the more value you can offer your customers.

c) Goal Setting: Set yourself lofty but doable goals. Create an action plan and break them down into smaller milestones. Review your progress on a regular basis and make improvements as needed. Setting specific goals will help you stay focused and motivated, propelling you to accomplishment.

c) Collaboration and Mentorship: Surround yourself with others who share your enthusiasm for sales excellence. Collaborate with your coworkers, solicit input, and learn from their experiences. Develop ties with mentors who can offer advice and assist you navigate obstacles along the road.

3. The Art of Closing a Sale: The final stage of a successful sales process is closing a sale. Consider the following methods to get closer to being a master:

a) Active Listening: Pay close attention to your prospect's wants and worries. Tailor your pitch to their individual needs, addressing their concerns and giving answers. You boost the odds of a successful close by proving that you understand their specific position.

b) Dealing with Objections: Objections are an inevitable element of the sales process. Anticipate frequent concerns and plan compelling responses ahead of time.

Empathize with objections, clear up misunderstandings, and reframe objections as possibilities for mutually beneficial solutions.

b) Self-assurance and Persistence: Self-assurance is contagious and inspires trust in your clientele. Believe in the value you offer and communicate it truthfully. Maintain persistence and a cheerful attitude even when faced with rejection. Follow up with prospects to show your dedication to finding the best solution for them.

Sales is an art form that can be mastered with effort, ongoing study, and the development of vital abilities. You may put yourself on the route to success by focusing on relationship building, product expertise, and effective communication. When you combine these pillars with a growth mentality, goal setting, cooperation, and a strategic approach to closing sales, you'll be positioned as a top performer in your office. Accept the adventure and its hardships.

CHAPTER 2

Targeting Your Audience

Even if you're not a big baseball fan, the iconic statement from Field of Dreams, "if you build it, they will come," has become an uplifting slogan about endurance, determination, and being open to whatever surprises the universe has in store for you. This formula can be used to create an effective marketing strategy. By "building" your target audience—identifying customer demographics and determining which tools would best attract them—"they" will arrive.

Rather than focusing on everyone, you should concentrate on the ideal customer for your company. Many small business owners make the mistake of believing that their product or service is appropriate for all customers. Targeting Facebook Ads to "all" (genders, ages, etc.) when your offering is clearly aimed at women over forty, for example, makes little sense. Advertising to everyone is rarely valid, and it can really harm your marketing efforts by upsetting individuals and wasting your advertising budget.

When determining your target audience, follow these steps:

1) Determine the demographics of your customers. Unless you're selling oxygen, your product or service isn't for everyone. So, who does it? Male or female? Are you old or young? Are you a conservative or a liberal? What are their socioeconomic status, educational level, and interests? Once you've narrowed the criteria, it'll be much easier to target your marketing plan to those who are most likely to benefit from what you're giving.

2) Determine your customer's requirements. Now that you've identified the type of individual you'll be targeting, you'll need to determine their unique wants in the context of what your company offers. In other words, what is the problem that your product or service solves for them? By putting yourself in their shoes and anticipating their inquiries, you'll be able to address their concerns in your response—your marketing message—before they arise.

The demographics of the various social networks are broken down by LinkedIn:

Facebook has 1.32 billion members, both male and female, aged 18 to 54, and more interested in consumer items than luxury goods.

Twitter has 271 million users, predominantly men between the ages of 18 and 29, who want to acquire their news through this network.

LinkedIn has 300 million users, both male and female, aged 30-64, who are well-educated professionals with respectable earnings.

Pinterest has 70 million users, the majority of whom are female and between the ages of 18 and 49, and are interested in food, drink, and family/parenting material. A powerful platform for visual products and services.

Instagram has 200 million users, the majority of which are females aged 18 to 29, and who are interested in fashion, accessories, and entertainment-related topics. Very good for graphic marketing, similar to Pinterest.

3) Purchase internet advertisements. Online advertising should be part of your marketing strategy if you have the means, but choose a platform where your target buyers spend their time. Their business boundaries, according to ping. Co-marketing with pre- and post-natal fitness establishments, for example, can help both organizations without diverting customers away from either. You can guest write on each other's blogs, share social media postings, co-host contests and giveaways, and provide special discount codes to each other's customers.

4) Promote social networking in the workplace. Sharing is at the heart of the new online landscape. Diamond Strategic Marketing recommends that the entire team, not just the marketing folks, be involved in outreach since it can lead to actual, personal "marketing" of your company's product or service (provided your employees enjoy and utilize what you're selling).

While most workplaces frown on online networking, Robert Nolte, VP of business development at EveryoneSocial, believes it is beneficial since "every employee has a voice and an audience." They will want to talk about the product if they actually believe in it, so take advantage of this word-of-mouth advertising.

CHAPTER 3

Building Trust

How to Win the Trust of Your Customers

Here are seven critical actions your organization can do to establish client trust:

1. Create an excellent product.

The first step in establishing client trust is to provide an excellent product. Consider your target clients' wants and design products or services to meet them. Make items that are simple and pleasurable to use for your clients, as this will increase their likelihood of engaging with your organization in the future and becoming repeat customers.

Another important aspect of earning customer trust is demonstrating your company's principles. You can make a statement outlining your company's values and then conduct activities that reflect those principles. Your firm can appear more authentic to customers and create trust by reflecting its ideals via its activities.

2. Develop strong customer ties.

The next step in establishing customer trust is to establish strong customer connections. Developing strong customer relationships entails the following:

Making a connection: Making a connection with clients is a crucial aspect of developing strong relationships with them. This could be accomplished through a sales pitch, an advertisement, or another method. Gaining their attention and personalizing your engagement with them is the key to engaging with them.

Empathy: Demonstrating empathy to clients is an excellent method to improve customer connections. This might demonstrate to clients that your organization understands them and wants to assist them.

Maintaining great customer connections necessitates frequent and effective communication. Email, social media, and other channels can be used for relationship-building communication.

expressing gratitude: By expressing gratitude to customers, your organization may enhance its customer ties even further. consumers are more inclined to engage with your firm in the future and become loyal consumers as a result of this.

Obtaining client feedback: By soliciting feedback from your consumers, you may demonstrate to them that your organization values their thoughts and input. You can solicit feedback by sending out surveys via email or by including pop-up surveys on your website. Include a section where customers can submit unique feedback and suggestions. Then you may make improvements that will improve your firm and reflect the feedback you received from your clients.

3. Be open and honest.

Maintaining consumer trust requires transparency. It entails being transparent and honest with clients so that they may comprehend your company's actions. Transparency can include the following:

Publishing thorough product information, such as materials and chemicals

demonstrating how your organization works behind the scenes

Responding to consumer suggestions and complaints

Featuring firm employees' stories

Transparency with your customers can give them the impression that your organization is trustworthy, which can increase customer trust. It can also provide them with insight into your company's processes, making them feel more engaged.

4. Assist customers in resolving issues.

Another critical aspect in establishing and keeping consumer confidence is assisting clients in resolving issues through good customer service. If a consumer has a problem with your product or service, make a commitment to resolving it. Try to fix their difficulties as swiftly as possible while demonstrating empathy and kindness. Excellent customer service involves the following:

Customers can contact with customer support agents through a variety of means.

Customer service agents provide prompt and consistent responses.

Individual solutions to individual challenges

Customer service workers must have compassionate and understanding attitudes.

A positive customer service experience can increase client trust and make them more willing to engage with your firm in the future.

5. Display good customer feedback and testimonials

Positive customer evaluations and testimonials are another approach to increase customer confidence. Reviews and testimonials can be posted on your website, blog, or social media. If you have individual customers who have had positive experiences with your firm, you may contact them personally to inquire about generating a testimonial video or blog post for them. Highlighting positive comments from actual consumers might increase the likelihood that other customers would trust your company. The publication of client evaluations and testimonials might boost your company's credibility.

6. Keep your company's reputation intact.
Keeping a positive company reputation is essential for earning client trust. Maintaining your company's reputation entails numerous aspects, such as meeting high quality standards and employing and developing excellent people. Maintaining these standards over time can help you maintain your reputation and client trust.

CHAPTER 4

Crafting Compelling Offers

If you want to build an offer that can sell on autopilot, you must first understand your ideal demographics, business climate, and competition. While it may appear complicated at first, the components of an appealing offer are relatively simple.

Keep in mind that this talk assumes you understand a few other critical ideas, such as sales funnels, email sequences, and online marketing methods and techniques that will assist you in increasing exposure and driving visitors. Once that traffic arrives, your enticing offer will assist in converting those so-called "window shoppers" into consumers.

The keys to creating a convincing proposition.

There are seven crucial components to creating a captivating and enticing offer. They are all significant. Each of these must exist if you are serious about success in business. If you ignore any of these seven keys, you will be primarily squandering your time and will not attain any kind of success.

Alternatively, if you pay attention to these seven keys, you can expect your offer to become saturated over time and to succeed. While the keys give the foundation, it is up to you to execute. Take the time to fully comprehend and implement your offer, and you'll be well on your way to market dominance.

1. Be specific.

The first stage in developing an attractive offer is to be absolutely clear about what you're selling. People who are perplexed will not buy from you. This is where your copywriting abilities will be put to use. If you want people to buy from you, make sure you build and give a very clear and readily understood offer.

The simplest approach to accomplish this is to accurately represent and communicate the objective of whatever you're selling. Please be specific. Use clear language that accurately describe the offer. Use figures, dates, or percentages to depict specifics of the deal while ensuring that the title is engaging, relevant to your audience, and makes a promise that can be fulfilled through whatever you're selling.

2. Provide excellent value.

In business, value has become less common. Most people want to perform the least amount of labor for the most reward when it should be the contrary. You must provide enormous levels of value in whatever you are offering. If you're just putting something up and hoping to make a lot of money, you could get some sales at first, but don't anticipate any consistency if your value falls short.

Offers that do not provide value will be mostly refunded, denied, or contested. That headache on your shoulders is not something you desire. You don't want bad or negative press or reviews. If you go out of your way to provide enormous amounts of value, your offer will snowball. Remember that word-of-mouth travels like wildfire. And unfavorable exposure might ruin your company for good.

3. Provide a discount or premium.

You must give your customers a cause to buy from you right away. To accomplish so, you must either give a significant discount or a premium. What extras can you add to the offer to make it extremely impossible to pass up? Give this some serious thinking. Remember that the prospect's information and attention span are extremely limited. If they have an issue, you may not be able to readily overcome it unless you offer a premium service or a discount. It's not about offering rock-bottom costs; it's about making the deal irresistible by piling on the goodies.

4. Describe your offer.

People are inherently skeptical. People will need to be convinced when they come across your offer, regardless of who you are or what you're selling. Whether or not you've developed a good relationship with that person through time, you must provide a very clear justification for your offer. What will it do for the prospect? What will they be able to accomplish after purchasing it?

It's hardly rocket science, but it does necessitate careful communication. As indicated in the first key, the offer must be very apparent, but it must also be thoroughly described. Make use of bullet points that are loaded with buyer psychology and attractive sales content. Your goal here isn't to mislead people into buying, but to convince them that they must have what you're providing.

5. Demand an immediate response.

Demand a quick response from your prospect. There must be some form of scarcity theory applied here. Perhaps the offer will expire in a few days or hours. Perhaps there are just a limited number of whatever you're offering. Perhaps it's something else. Whatever it is, you must insist on a response right now. Make it clear that time is of the essence. Because you may never see them again if they leave. Why do you believe auto salespeople strive so hard to encourage you to buy right away? They understand that if you quit, your chances of securing that transaction plunge.

6. Include a clear call to action.
Your offer must feature a powerful call to action. Inform the prospect of your expectations. Consider them to be a 10-year-old youngster who has to be instructed on the following steps. You've probably seen this on the most enticing deals, where it instructs you what to do next. For instance, click on the green "buy now" button, enter your information, and then download the product. Or something along those lines.
Use large, bold colors and buttons, and limit the number of clickable components on a website. Remember, you want to steer the prospect in the right path without overwhelming them with options. This is also why you should remove navigation and menus from offer pages.

7. Provide a fail-safe guarantee.
If you want your offer to succeed and sell on autopilot, provide the prospect an ironclad guarantee and reverse any risk involved. When the prospect believes there is no danger involved, this will compel them to act. This is why you see 30-day money-back guarantees on almost everything you buy. Smart marketers understand the significance of delivering these promises.
Simply take the risk out of the customer's hands and place it in yours. This also demonstrates how certain you are that the buyer would like whatever you have to give.

CHAPTER 5

Handling Objections

What is the significance of objection handling?

Various Types of Sales Objections

How to Overcome Sales Obstacles

Common Sales Refusals

What exactly is a sales objection?

A sales objection is any concern a prospect expresses about a barrier impeding their ability to buy from you - an unambiguous indication that you need to address more areas of the buying process than you anticipated.

A common sales objection originates from a buyer's "lack" of a particular capability. Prospects object to a sale when they believe they do not have the means, interest, need, or ability to purchase from you at the time.

While objections are one of the more difficult and irritating aspects of sales, they are not necessarily dead ends. Let's take a closer look at how you can avoid these potential stumbling blocks.

What exactly is objection handling?

When a prospect expresses a concern about the product/service that a salesperson is selling, the salesperson replies in a way that alleviates those fears and allows the deal to proceed. Typically, objections revolve around price, product fit, or competitors. Sometimes the objection is as simple as a dismissal.

Responding to the buyer in a way that changes their mind or alleviates their anxieties is what objection handling entails.

Some salespeople quarrel with their prospects or try to bully them into backing down, but this isn't proper objection handling. Prospects are usually more convinced than ever of their viewpoint in these situations, and salespeople end up eroding the trust and rapport they've built with them.

Instead of telling your prospect they're incorrect, assist them in reaching a new conclusion on their own. And if you can't persuade them, it's a solid indication they're not a good fit.

It's also critical to differentiate between sales objections and brush-offs. While complaints are genuine, dismissals are excuses. Consider an objection to be "I see the value in your product, but I'm not sure about buying it for X reason," but a brush-off is "I don't want to talk to you."

Objections are significantly more serious than dismissals.

Object Resolution

Handling objections is a normal and frustrating part of the sales process. Carrying out the process necessitates certain activities and skills that every salesman should be familiar with. These include being aware of your surroundings, gathering background information, leading with empathy, and asking intelligent, open-ended questions.

Being aware of your surroundings

There is no one-size-fits-all objection-handling method that can address every worry a prospect may have. You must be aware of where you are in the sales process, the kind of the deal you are pursuing, and the prospect's demands and interests, among other things.

Understanding the conditions that shape a prospect's objections is critical to effectively addressing them. That is why, as your talks with each prospect proceed, you must keep situational awareness.

Obtaining Comprehensive Background Information

This point follows naturally from the previous one: substantial background information informs effective, actionable situational awareness. Investigate your prospect's company and, to some extent, the prospect themselves.

What are the company's current challenges? What problems do the prospect's colleagues in the industry have on a regular basis? If you've previously worked with similar-sized firms, try to recollect the concerns they raised.

And, in the event of your contact, be aware of their responsibilities. What is the scope of their decision-making authority? What areas of the business do they deal with on a daily basis? What are the most common issues that people in their job face?

If you know all of this and more, you'll be in a good position to answer objections gracefully.

Empathy-Based Leadership

Objections are a normal part of the sales process, and in many, if not most, cases, they reflect legitimate concerns. That is why, when your prospects push back, you must avoid being visibly upset and impatient with them.

Every great sales effort begins with empathy. You should not sell to a prospect solely to make money; rather, you should sell to them because your product or service is best suited to their pain points. As a result, you must always keep their wants and interests in mind.

If you stay on top of their concerns and situations — and approach them with compassion and understanding — you may set yourself up to anticipate and effectively address any objections they may have.

Posing Inquisitive, Open-Ended Questions

Every other element on this list can be emphasized by the capacity to ask meaningful, open-ended questions. If you want to grasp and efficiently resolve your prospect's objections, you must first understand their pain areas.

This frequently begins with asking pertinent, courteous questions and allowing them ample time to respond. Avoid one-word, "yes or no" replies to queries, and don't be hesitant to use silence to your advantage.

Allow your buyers to express themselves. Feel out their anxieties — and position yourself to anticipate any objections they may offer.

ThBonding Process® is an effective method for handling objections.

Carew International's LAER: The Bonding Process is a tried-and-true strategy for resolving objections. Listen, Acknowledge, Explore, and Respond are the four steps in LAER.

When faced with an objection, the first step is to listen to it. This shows your customer that you are concerned about their concerns and are interested in what they have to say.

The following stage is to recognize your customer's concern. This is where you show that you've been paying attention. An acknowledgement might be as basic as a head nod or reiterating the issue. A genuine acknowledgement can avoid an argument and be relaxing. Sometimes all your customers want to know is that they have been heard.

The third stage is to investigate the factors that are driving your customer's complaint. It is critical that you fully get what your customer meant by what they stated.

For example, your customer may have expressed a price concern, but the true reason they don't want to engage with you is that they like the competition's salesperson and appreciate their attention.

If you do not investigate the customer's objection, you will not discover that they are using "price" as a smokescreen and will be unable to reply correctly.

"The cliche 'people buy from those they know, like, and trust' still holds true. Buyers desire (and anticipate) a personalized sales experience. "How you present yourself and your product either builds trust — or gives your competitors a foot in the door," said Qwilr Co-Founder Mark Tanner.

Responding is the final stage. Only when you fully comprehend your customer's objection can you respond with a recommendation, an alternative, a solution, or a next step tailored to solve the customer's worry and close the sale.

Sales professionals do not have to go through objection handling. Instead, use objections as chances to assist your consumer and strengthen your relationship with them.

LAER from Carew International: The Bonding Process® is a powerful strategy for dealing with objections that results in a good, two-way transaction between the salesperson and the customer.

What is the significance of objection handling?

Nothing is more harmful to a deal than leaving sales objections unresolved until the very end. The longer a customer maintains an idea, the stronger that opinion normally is – and the more difficult it is to oppose.

With this in mind, rather than avoiding objections, welcome them. You can also find them proactively by asking questions like, "Do you have any concerns about X?"

"Are there any obstacles that would stop you from buying?"

"How confident are you that [product] will be a success?" Why?"

"You appear to be concerned about X. "What do you think?"

Various Types of Sales Objections

As I mentioned at the start of this post, most sales objections spring from a "lack" – and they usually come from a sensible place. Prospects that raise objections typically state that they simply cannot buy right now.

However, those "lacks" are frequently misplaced, and if you know what you're doing, you can generally work around them. Let's take a closer look at some of the most frequent kinds of sales objections.

Various Sales Objections

Budget constraints

a lack of faith

Lack of Demand

Lack of Immediacy

A successful sale occurs when the product or service you sell is within the prospect's budget, you have the authority to persuade them, they need the service or product, and the moment is correct. This phenomena is known as BANT (Budget, Authority, Need, and Timing). Determining BANT should be a standard component of your qualification process.

It follows that sales objections would be the inverse of BANT:

1. Budget constraints

"It's too expensive."

The most common objections are those based on price. This is due to the fact that all purchases involve some level of financial risk.

As a sales representative, you should think about the positioning of your product or service and how to illustrate its value. This shifts the discussion to risk versus reward.

They can be persuaded that the risk is worth taking if you provide value and paint a picture of where your solution will take them.

2. a lack of faith

"I've never heard of your company."

People do business with people they like, recognize, and believe in.

In an inbound sales interaction, the prospect has most certainly interacted with your content or is familiar with your company in some way. This obstacle could be overcome by reviving their memory, or you could think about your sales cycle and whether you can nurture them through it. However, not all discussions are inbound, and they may have never heard of you. At this point, you should increase the value you deliver with your elevator pitch. Make a point of emphasizing your company's market authority.

3. Lack of Demand

"I don't see how this can help me."

On the surface, this appears to be an objection, but it is actually a chance to provide information to the prospect (and receive information from them in return). To qualify the prospect and assess their needs, use open-ended and layered inquiries. If you find a match, use it to demonstrate value.

4. Lack of Immediacy

"[X problem] isn't important for me right now."

The idea here is to determine whether timing is an issue or if the prospect is dismissing you. One method is to ask them to explain on why it isn't important or what alternative concerns are now occupying their attention.

Listen carefully to see if their explanation comprises specific time concerns or generic justifications. You might have an opening if they're doing backflips to explain inaction on a true pain area.

If all else fails, make a later appointment with them to discuss the problem further.

How to Overcome Sales Obstacles

Active listening should be practiced.

What you hear, repeat back.

Confirm your prospect's concerns.

Pose follow-up inquiries.

Make use of social proof.

Make a note of a specific date and time to follow up.

Prepare for sales objections.

When attempting to exceed sales objectives, it is critical that you answer effectively and avoid reacting rashly to your prospect's arguments. Here are some effective ways for

1. Active listening should be practiced.

First and foremost, while your prospect shares their worries with you, make sure you are actively listening to what they are saying.

While your prospect is expressing their concerns, listen to comprehend rather than respond. Avoid interrupting them while they are speaking, and allow them to openly express their concerns and criticisms.

2. What you hear, repeat back.

After your prospect has presented their objections, repeat what you heard to ensure you understood accurately. This will not only help you explain their ideas, but it will also make your prospect feel heard and respected, which is essential for creating trust.

3. Confirm your prospect's concerns.

After confirming that you understand where your prospect is coming from, continue to create trust by empathizing with them and affirming their point of view. No, this does not imply that you must disparage your product or endorse a competitor.

For example, if you're selling automation software and your prospect is concerned about their ability to integrate your software into their complex system, you could tell them, "I understand, implementing new software can feel like a daunting task. Thankfully, we have an incredible tech team that has experience working with similar organizations, and can handle a seamless transition for you."

With this reaction, you acknowledge that their complaint is real and offer a remedy to alleviate their concerns.

4. Pose follow-up inquiries.

When you hear objectives, you want to do everything you can to keep the conversation flowing naturally. If you notice your prospect withdrawing, asking follow-up questions is a good method to keep them chatting.

Don't ask questions that have a straightforward "yes" or "no" answer. Make sure to ask open-ended questions that allow your prospect to continue discussing your product. The more information they provide, the more options you have to potentially turn the deal around.

5. Make use of social proof.

Sharing the tale of another customer who had similar worries and went on to see success with your product can be a good strategy, depending on the nature of your prospect's issue.

If you're in B2B sales, you can also give pertinent information about your prospect's competitors, as well as any success they've had in overcoming a comparable obstacle.

6. Make a note of a specific date and time to follow up.

If your prospect requests additional time to consider their alternatives, give them the time and space they need. But you don't want to abandon them. Set a definite time and date to follow up soon so that too much time passes, and offer to answer any questions they have in the meanwhile while they deliberate.

7. Prepare for sales objections.

Finally, the most effective technique for dealing with sales objections is to anticipate them. When you're prepared for objections, you're lot less likely to be thrown off guard.

When objections arise, having a set of neutral recommendations to provide prospects can help keep sales moving. Because you listened to the consumer and investigated their reasoning rather than responding in haste, they're usually prepared to hear you out if you have a solution.

Keeping track of the most common objections you receive is also beneficial. You may commit more time to rehearsing and polishing your responses once you know what to expect.

We also urge that sales representatives practice role-playing to improve their objection-handling skills. Take turns with another team member expressing common objections (such as any of the 40 on this list), replying, and providing feedback.

Now that you understand what objection management is, why it is important, and how to improve, let's look at the top 40 sales objections.

Common Sales Refusals

It's prohibitively pricey.

There isn't any money.

We don't have any money left over.

This budget must be used elsewhere.

I don't want to be tied down by a contract.

We already have another vendor on board.

I'm under contract with a competitor.

I can find a cheaper version somewhere.

I'm pleased with your rival.

[False assertion regarding your product] states competitor X.

I'm not authorized to approve this.

I'm not going to be able to sell this internally.

[Economic customer] is not persuaded.

We're being downsized/purchased.

There is simply too much going on right now.

I'm a member of a purchasing group.

I'm not familiar with your company.

We're doing fantastic in this regard.

We don't have a business plan yet.

It's just not necessary right now.

I don't see how your product can help me.

I'm not sure I comprehend your product.

I've heard negative things about you from [business].

We do not have the resources to put the product into action.

Your product is simply very complicated.

You don't grasp my difficulties. I require assistance with Y, not X.

You have no idea what I'm talking about.

Your product lacks X feature, which we require.

We're content with the way things are.

I don't see any ROI potential.

It's only a passing fad.

Your product is incompatible with our present setup.

Your product seems fantastic, but I'm currently overburdened.

Click

I'm currently preoccupied.

I'm uninterested.

Just email me some details.

Please contact me again in the fourth quarter.

How did you obtain my contact information?

I despise you.

These decisions are not my responsibility.

Is your product capable of X, Y, or Z?

I'm sorry, but I have to cancel. I'll get back to you at a more convenient time.

Hello, you have arrived at [Prospect's Name]...

No is a common response among salespeople. Actually, 60% of buyers say no four times before saying yes. Objections differ depending on the size of the firm, the industry, and what you're selling. Knowing and preparing for the most typical objections, on the other hand, will help you close more deals.

If you have a costly product, money, budget, and pricing will most likely be an issue. If you're in a competitive market, your opponents may be other sellers. Timing and haste are also frequent issues.

Every remark and gesture in sales helps to develop relationships. Before you can actively listen, share data, or validate a prospect's viewpoint, you must first gain their permission.

The responses below can help you respond to the most common objections you'll hear on your first few calls with a prospect. However, the most efficient technique to deal with criticisms is to create your own responses.

Featured instrument:

You're presumably already aware of this. However, you are aware that writing is a difficult ability to master. Many salespeople flourish over the phone or in a meeting but struggle to put their ideas on paper.

So, if you want to get started quickly and easily, check out this. It includes essential templates to help you get started with your unique objection responses.

Price and Budget Objections from Sales

1. "It's too expensive."

Price objections are the most typical sort of objection, and they are even raised by prospects who intend to buy. Beware: if you start emphasizing on price as a selling element, you become a transactional intermediary. Instead, return to the product's worth.

Example of a Rebuttal

"I'd love to unpack [product's] features and how it can help with the issue of [prospect problem] you shared with me."

2. "There's no money."

It's possible that your prospect's company isn't large enough or making enough money right now to justify purchasing your goods. Track their progress and consider how you might assist your prospect in getting to the point where your solution would fit into their business.

Example of a Rebuttal

"I understand. Allow me to explain our other offerings that may be a better fit for your current growth levels and budget."

3. "We don't have any budget left this year."

A variation on the "no money" objection, your prospect is telling you that they are experiencing cash flow problems. However, if there is a critical issue, it must be addressed as soon as possible. Help your prospect obtain a budget from executives to purchase now, or set up a follow-up contact for when they expect funding to return.

Example of a Rebuttal

"Let's schedule a follow-up call for when you expect funding to return. When do you think that may be?"

4. "We need to use that budget somewhere else."

Prospects will occasionally try to earmark resources for other purposes. It is your responsibility to make your product/service a priority that requires immediate funding allocation. Share with you case studies of similar businesses that have saved money, boosted efficiency, or had a big ROI.

Example of a Rebuttal

"We had a customer with a similar issue, but by purchasing [product] they were actually able to increase their ROI and assign some of their new revenue to other parts of the budget."

5. "I don't want to get stuck in a contract."

A prospect who rejects time-based contract conditions despite a genuine need and interest is often hesitant for cash flow considerations. Fortunately, there are solutions — see if you can provide monthly or quarterly payments instead of asking for a year or more commitment up front.

Example of a Rebuttal

"I understand. Let's talk about some different contract terms and payment schedules that I can offer you. Perhaps these would be a better fit."

Objections to the Competition in Sales

6. "We're already working with [Vendor X]."

A prospect who is already working with a competition can be a valuable resource. They've already identified a need and developed a solution; much of the instruction you'd be responsible for has already been completed. You can spend your time doing what you would have to put off with a prospect who hasn't identified their problem yet — talking about your product.

Simply because a prospect is working with a competitor does not imply that they are satisfied with them. Investigate the relationship and pay close attention to problems that could be resolved with your product.

Example of a Rebuttal

"Why did you choose [vendor]? What's working well? What's not? Allow me to explain how [product] is different."

7. "I'm locked into a contract with a competitor."

This sentence is constructed in a way that advertises your prospect's sense of being imprisoned, making it one of the easiest competitor-related objections to resolve. See if you can devise a creative discount to offset the expense of terminating a contract early, or show ROI that will compensate for the sunk cost.

Of again, your candidate could simply have used an unnecessarily unfavorable phrase. Inquire about their relationship with the competitor to assess whether they are truly satisfied or eager to switch vendors.

Example of a Rebuttal

"How is your relationship with [competitor]? Perhaps I can offer a discount to make up for the cost of switching over to work with us."

8. "I can get a cheaper version of your product somewhere else."

Find out what you're up against here. Are you in a competitive situation where the prospect is pitting you against a competition in order to increase the discount? Is your prospect under the notion that a similar, less expensive product will suffice?

If the former, state your deepest discount and stress the attributes that distinguish your goods. If they ask you to go lower, walk away. Take advantage of the comparison in the second situation. Play highlight the distinctions and stress overall worth rather than cost.

Example of a Rebuttal

"What are the points of differentiation between [product] and your other option? What gives you the most value and support?"

9. "I'm happy with [Competitor X]."

What if your prospect is content? The same method applies – find out why they think their connection with your rival is valuable, and discover areas where your product may improve.

Example of a Rebuttal

"That's great. What components of the product or relationship are you most satisfied with? I'd love to learn more and see how we may compare."

10. "Competitor X says [false statement about your product]."

Salespeople, according to the founder of Your Sales MBA, should initially answer with "That's not true," then pause.

According to Hoffman, 90% of the time, this response will satisfy the customer and they will move on. You'll appear calm and collected, whilst your opponent will appear desperate and insecure.

If your prospect remains uncertain, they will ask another question. You can then provide more context in your rebuttal.

Example of a Rebuttal

"We manufacture our products in Canada, not Thailand. I have a map of our factories and distribution routes if you'd like to see it."

Sales Objections Regarding Authority or Purchase Ability

11. "I'm not authorized to sign off on this purchase."

No worries. Ask your prospect for the name of the appropriate person to speak with, and then transfer your call to them.

Example of a Rebuttal

"Who is the right person to speak to regarding this purchase? Can you redirect me to them, please?"

12. "I can't sell this internally."

Your prospect may not be able to do so, but you can. After all, you market your goods on a daily basis. Ask your prospect what objections they expect and assist them in developing a business case for adopting your solution. Check with Marketing to see if there is any collateral you can use on behalf of your prospect.

Example of a Rebuttal

"What objections do you think you'll face? Can I help you prepare the business case for when you speak with your decision-makers? I may have some enablement materials I can share to help."

13. "[Economic buyer] isn't convinced."

If you've already answered point #12 by offering internal resources, and your prospect still can't get it, it's time to walk away. While it's heartbreaking to give up on a prospect who is on your side but can't persuade the higher-ups, it's also a waste of time to keep arguing with someone who will never see the worth of your product.

Example of a Rebuttal

"That's too bad. If anything changes, please don't hesitate to contact me. I'd love to help you get your team onboard."

14. "We're being downsized / bought out."

This happens infrequently, but when it does, there is usually little you can do about it. There is no transaction if there is no company. Wrap the relationship professionally so that when your prospect finds a new job, they are more likely to restart the dialogue with a new employer.

Example of a Rebuttal

"Thank you for your time and for speaking with me regarding this product. If you're ever in need of [product or service], please don't hesitate to contact me."

15. "There's too much going on right now."

Request that your prospect clarify their competing priorities for you. If they can't, it's probably a brush-off, and you should question them about why they don't want to interact with you.

Don't worry if they can provide concrete solutions. Set a follow-up meeting time and send along helpful resources in the meantime to stay on your prospect's radar.

Example of a Rebuttal

"I understand. What are some of your competing priorities? I'd love to schedule a follow-up call for when your calendar clears up."

16. "I'm part of a buying group."

Buying groups allow independent businesses to band together and make joint purchases from vendors, usually at a far lower price than they could acquire on their own.

If your organization is not on a prospect's approved supplier list, your prospect is unlikely to be interested. After all, you can't give them the same price if they buy in volume.

Respond to this objection by researching their membership data. When you've learned more, you'll be able to determine whether it makes economic sense for this prospect to deal with you — and whether there's a chance to become one of their buying group's vendors.

Example of a Rebuttal

"Are there limits on whom you can buy from? What price are you currently receiving? What companies belong to your buying coalition?"

Objections to Need and Fit in Sales

17. "I've never heard of your company."

Consider this objection to be a request for information. Instead of an elevator pitch, provide a brief explanation of your value proposition.

Example of a Rebuttal

"We're a company that sells ad space on behalf of publishers like yourself. I'd love to speak with you about your revenue model and see if we can help."

18. "We're doing great in X area."

If you hear this objection, ask a few more clarifying questions and qualify a bit more.

Example of a Rebuttal

"What are your goals? How much progress has been made?"

19. "We don't have that business pain."

This objection is frequently raised as a dismissal or because prospects haven't realized they have a problem yet. And, while you may eventually discover that they do not require your product, do not take this objection at its value.

Example of a Rebuttal

"Interesting. What solutions are you currently using to address that area of your business?"

20. "X problem isn't important right now."

A simple "Oh?" might sometimes elicit a response from your prospect. Listen carefully for genuine reasons for the need's low priority rather than cliches. Remember that excuses can indicate that your prospect is aware of a problem and is attempting to justify their inaction. Take advantage of this and instill a sense of urgency.

Example of a Rebuttal

"Tell me more about that. What are your current priorities?"

21. "I don't see what your product could do for me."

Another information request disguised as an objection. Reiterate the objectives or issues you've mentioned, and explain how your product may help solve specific problems.

Example of a Rebuttal

"Interesting. Can you share what specific challenges you're facing right now? Perhaps [product] presents a solution we have yet to discuss."

22. "I don't understand your product."

If your prospect can't get their head around your offering, that's a red flag. If your product is exceptionally complicated or specialized, it may be time to dismiss your prospect in order to avoid churning in two months.

But don't give up right away. Inquire with your prospect about the components of your product that they are uncertain about, and then try describing it in a different way. Bring in a technician or product engineer to answer questions that are outside your scope.

Example of a Rebuttal

"What aspects of the product are confusing to you? I'd love to connect you to a customer success technician or product engineer to help you better understand how we can help you."

23. "I've heard complaints about you from [company]."

Word-of-mouth recommendations are extremely potent, which can be both a blessing and a curse. Instead of defending your solution, business, or brand, which will just validate the criticism, thank them for providing input. Then follow up with a value-added offer.

This allows you to develop credibility and trust with your prospect. When you provide them with a positive experience, they will automatically build a favorable opinion of you.

Example of a Rebuttal

"Thanks for sharing that feedback with me. I'll pass it along to [relevant department]. While we're on the phone, would you be interested in hearing a few tips for improving your average invoicing turnaround time?"

24. "We don't have capacity to implement the product."

This objection has the potential to be a deal breaker. Depending on the product you sell, your prospect may need to increase staff or divert resources to fully benefit from your offering, and if they actually aren't able to, you may have to exclude them.

Another strategy is to examine your prospect's existing obligations and day-to-day activities to discover what job responsibilities could be eliminated or simplified by your product.

Example of a Rebuttal

"I hear you, and I want [product] to add value, not take it away. What are your current day-to-day responsibilities in your job? I'd love to explain how the product, once onboarded, can alleviate some of those problems."

25. "Your product is too complicated."

Determine whether your prospect is perplexed by specific aspects or whether the product is genuinely beyond their comprehension. If it's the latter, you may have to rule that lead out. If it's the latter, remind your prospect that if they decide to buy, they'll have access to your customer support staff and that you'll be available to address any implementation questions they have.

Example of a Rebuttal

"What features are confusing to you? Remember, our customer service team will be available 'round-the-clock to help with implementation."

26. "You don't understand my challenges. I need help with Y, not X."

It's crucial to make your prospect feel heard. Restate your impression of their situation, then align with your prospect's take and move forward from there. A lot of misunderstandings and hard feelings can be resolved simply by rephrasing your prospect's words.

Example of a Rebuttal

"Please accept my apologies!" Allow me to reiterate my understanding of your problems, and please let me know if I'm missing anything or misstating anything."

27. *"You don't understand my business."*

If you sell to a certain industry, you probably know something about your prospect's company. Inform them that you have previous experience dealing with similar firms and solving similar difficulties.

If you just made a mistake about your prospect's company or industry, don't be scared to admit it. Your openness will be appreciated by your prospects.

Example of a Rebuttal

"I'm sorry — I assumed X was true, but it appears that it does not apply to your business."
"Could you please tell me a little bit more about X?"

28. *"Your product doesn't have X feature, and we need it."*

Consider recommending a complementary product that can be used in conjunction with yours. However, if that specific requirement is critical and your solution cannot meet it, your prospect may not be a good fit. It's time to disqualify and move on to a more suitable opportunity.

Example of a Rebuttal

"Have you looked into [partner or related product]?" It is compatible with ours and can be used in conjunction with it to solve for Y."

29. *"We're happy the way things are."*

Perhaps everything is going swimmingly. But, more than likely, your prospect is facing a hurdle (after all, who isn't?). Do some light qualifying to see if they have any issues you can help them with, then move forward or disqualify based on their responses.

Example of a Rebuttal

"That's fantastic! "Could you please explain how you're currently solving for X?"

30. "I don't see the potential for ROI."

This indicates that you will need to produce a formal pitch for either your contact or their managers, based on internal figures from your prospect or customer case studies. Nothing sells better than hard numbers.

Example of a Rebuttal

"I'd be delighted to show you. Can we set up a time for me to explain our product's ability to provide you and your team with a strong ROI?"

31. "X is just a fad."

This objection may be raised if your product introduces a new notion to your prospect's sector. For example, social media is now universally acknowledged as an essential component of a solid corporate strategy, when many would have laughed at it seven years ago.

This is the time to bring out any testimonials or client case studies you have to demonstrate the ROI of your solution. If you're introducing a new notion or practice, you must demonstrate that it works.

Example of a Rebuttal

"I understand why you could believe that. Let's set up a time for me to go over how our product has helped other firms like yours succeed with X — and why it's here to stay."

32. "Your product doesn't work with our current [tools, set-up]."

If the customer is wedded to their current solutions, this objection can be a deal breaker. However, your product may eventually replace or render these tools obsolete. A workaround may also be possible.

Ask some questions to find out.

Example of a Rebuttal

"What tools are you currently employing?" How important are those resources to your [strategy]? What do those items assist you with?"

33. "Your product sounds great, but I'm too swamped right now to handle [implementation, roll-out]."

Prospects are frequently turned off by the effort necessary to switch products, even if the ROI is significant.

To empathize with them, establish your credibility, and guarantee they have the capacity. Then, to overcome their aversion to change, delve into the costs or hardships of their current circumstance.

Calculate how much time, efficiency, money, or all of the above they stand to benefit.

Example of a Rebuttal

"I see what you're saying. It normally takes [X days/weeks] for our clients to become fully operational with [product]. "How many minutes do you spend per day on [task]?" Objections to Sales That Are Actually Brush-Offs

34. *Click.*"Don't worry if your prospect hangs up on you; *it happens to everyone eventually."*
Try contacting a different individual at the company via a different method.

You can also go on the offensive. Call back after a few seconds. Which technique you take is entirely dependent on how your chat with your prospect went before the phone call was disconnected.

Example of a Rebuttal

"Sorry, it appears that we have become disconnected!" "Do you have a few moments?"

35. *"I'm busy right now."*

Of course, your prospect is pressed for time; nearly every professional is these days. Simply clarify that you aren't looking for a full-fledged talk, but rather a quick chat about whether a longer discussion about your product would be a good fit at their firm.

Example of a Rebuttal

"I don't want to monopolize your time." Can we talk about your problems with X and how [product] can help?"

36. *"I'm not interested."*

It is far too early in a prospecting call for a prospect to indicate absolutely whether or not they are interested in your goods. Offer to send resources and set up a follow-up call.

Example of a Rebuttal

"I see what you're saying. Can we arrange for a follow-up call? Meanwhile, I can offer you some resources to help you learn more."

37. *"Just send me some information."*

This is an excellent time to introduce some qualification questions.

Example of a Rebuttal

"I'd be happy to send you some materials, but I want to make sure they're appropriate for you." "What topics are you curious about?"

38. *"Call me back next quarter."*

Prospects will frequently say this to discourage you from continuing the conversation. But don't let them get away with it – it's a hazy brush-off meant to make you fade away and disappear. Ask some probing inquiries to learn why they are dismissing you.

Example of a Rebuttal

"I'll follow up next quarter." Before we hang up, I'd like to hear about your upcoming quarter. Do you think you'll obtain approval from your bosses?"

39. "How did you get my information?"

Hopefully, you're not using numbers from lists obtained from the internet, since if you are, your prospects will be irritated. Don't be defensive; simply tell the prospect that they filled out a form on your website, signed up for additional information at a trade fair, or that you came across their website and wanted to connect to see if you might help.

Example of a Rebuttal

"I came across your website in my research and believe that [product] would be a great fit for you."

"I hate you."

40.*A disclaimer: In most cases, prospects will not mention this outright. It's also not required to become best friends with someone in order to market to them. If you and your prospect just don't get along, consider passing them off to a coworker to avoid losing the contract for good. What's the advantage? This objection is unrelated to your product or its worth.*

Example of a Rebuttal

"I'm sorry you're feeling this way. Can I pass the conversation along to my colleague [name]? Maybe he'll be a better fit."

41. "I'm not responsible for making these decisions."

This objection is intended to signal to your prospect that they are not the right person to have this conversation with. And, believe it or not, this is a quite typical event with unexpected rewards.

For one thing, the person you need to contact is most likely busy and won't have time to read their email, let alone schedule a demo with you. However, starting the conversation with someone on the team who has less authority can provide you with a direct introduction to the decision-maker. As a result, your sales process will go more swiftly than if you had targeted them from the start.

Example of a Rebuttal

"Hello [Name], thank you for informing me that you are not the appropriate person to discuss this with. Who makes these kinds of decisions on your team? "Could you please introduce me to them?"

42. "Does your product do X, Y, and Z?"

This is more of a roadblock to concluding a conversation with a prospect and getting them to the following appointment (such as a demo or a discovery call with the sales agent). However, it is one of the most common roadblocks that prevents an SDR from converting a lead into a SQL.

Not only does delving into the weeds waste time, but it also increases the likelihood of devolving into a features and benefits discussion when it isn't necessary. The good news is that this usually indicates that the prospect is intrigued. Use this chance to leave the topic on a positive note and to schedule another meeting to address it.

Example of a Rebuttal

43"I'm delighted you inquired. *I believe it will be beneficial to schedule a time when we can answer these and other questions with an expert. When would be a suitable time and day for us to talk?"*

"I'm sorry, but I have to cancel." I'll get back to you at a more convenient time."

People, including your prospects, dislike saying "No." This emerges as ghosting, procrastination (as already mentioned), and requesting more time.

Sales professionals swear on Sandler's method for dealing with difficult non-objection arguments like this. "You want to call out your prospect's lack of interest and get them to admit the answer is 'No' without going too negative," Rogewitz said. Here's how it works:

Prospect: "XYZ fluffy response."

"Typically, when I hear someone say XYZ, it really means ABC," says the salesperson. Is it reasonable to presume that's the case?"

You'll nudge your prospect into giving you the last answer you need to move forward by using this simple script.

Example of a Rebuttal

"When someone cancels and says they'll call me back, it usually means they're not interested in what I have to offer right now." Is it reasonable to presume that's the case?"

44. "Hello, you've reached [Prospect's Name] ..."

Is your prospect avoiding your calls like the plague? Do they take a long time to respond and always want approval? When you ask about the budget and priorities for the year, do they offer you imprecise answers?

You may be chatting with an individual contributor if you replied "Yes" to any of these questions. They aren't as comfortable on the phone as managers or decision-makers, they require a lot of internal approval, and they don't have access to critical financial information or company-wide priorities.

It's critical to acquire the trust of the gatekeeper and learn everything you can from them, but then you need to go on and create relationships with the individuals in the company who can actually choose your product or service.

Example of a Rebuttal

"Have you ever purchased this type of product or service before?" "Who will be in charge of this buying process?" "Who else should we bring on board for this conversation?"

Objections Will Help You Sell Better Objections are an unavoidable aspect of the sales process. Some are valid grounds to reject the prospect, while others are simply an attempt to dismiss you. However, if you are familiar with common concerns and are prepared to respond to them, you will be able to differentiate between prospects who have the potential to be good customers and prospects with whom you must part ways, allowing you to become a more efficient salesperson.

When an Objection Means No Prospects rarely give you the opportunity to explain the value that you can deliver. They are overworked and have little trust in the swarms of SDRs and sales reps who approach them on a daily basis.

Unfortunately, they've learned from experience that these knee-jerk objections are the strongest defenses against those who squander their time accidentally. As a result, as a salesperson, you must be more pushy and persistent.

That being said, at some point, no means no. The responses to the usual concerns listed above will help you cut through the reactionary objections prospects make without thinking. However, if you've said your piece and the prospect continues to object, let it go.

Nobody will buy without their will. Get as clear as possible on the objection and attempt to figure out what your prospect is actually worried about, but don't go beyond the prospect's comfort zone. As a general rule, if a possibility raises an objection twice, it is valid. No equals no.

As previously said, objection handling is vexing but unavoidable in sales. However, if you know how to get to the heart of your prospects' problems, lead with empathy, understand where most objections come from, and read these types of interactions correctly, you'll be in a strong position to deal with these concerns as they arise.

Overcoming Objections Can Become Your Most Valuable Sales Tool

As a sales professional, you'll hear no far more than yes. But that may be a lot of fun. Every no is a step closer to understanding more about your prospect and assisting them with the product or service you're selling.

Objection handling teaches you how to get to the heart of your prospects' problems. You can lead with empathy and understand where most objections are coming from with a little help. If you read these exchanges correctly, you'll be prepared to answer any objections that arise.

Editor's note: This post was first published in September 2015, but it has been updated for accuracy.

CHAPTER 6

Closing Deals

In 7 stages, learn how to complete a sales deal.

Every sales professional's ultimate goal is to close more sales.According to RAIN Sales Training research, top sales professionals not only achieve greater closure rates (48% versus 37%), but they also do so with fewer touches. You can do the same thing. Most of the time, it's a matter of fine-tuning your sales method, i.e.
Asking the appropriate questions
Highlighting the advantages of your product
Taking note of the alignment between product value and buyer goals
Instilling a sense of urgency
You may typically shorten the sales process and win more business by understanding the procedures to take to complete a contract.
We'll show you how to clinch a sales deal in seven stages (or less) in this guide. We'll also look at the varying needs for closing sales in various businesses, as well as some tried-and-true closing tactics.

Sales closing in 7 steps (or less)

You've chosen qualified leads and worked hard to understand their problems. You've used your best sales pitch, demo, or sales presentation to present a solution that will assist in resolving their issue and moving them down your sales funnel. It's now time to turn your prospect into a customer.

These seven steps will lead you through the fundamentals of finishing a conventional sales transaction.

1. Send the costs through

If you haven't yet discussed pricing in depth, the initial step should be to give your prospect an official sales proposal or quote. This is also an excellent moment to re-pitch your product or service by reviewing how it will benefit the buyer, particularly if the sales cycle has been lengthy or complicated.

Whenever feasible, provide your prospect a variety of pricing options. Offering a free test drive of your product can often assist seal the deal, especially in software and B2B sales.

If you're selling a SaaS subscription, you can have two or three different pricing options. According to consumer research, allowing your prospect to conduct a value comparison can satisfy their urge to shop about and speed up the decision-making process.

2. Request the sale

If you were thorough in your presentation and price, your prospect may be ready to buy right now. That is less likely if you do not actively ask for the sale during your sales call.

There are two major approaches to accomplish this.

In your proposal, add a clear call-to-action that encourages your prospect to click on their selected purchasing option and e-sign your contract.

You can set up a follow-up call or appointment to go over the pricing information you've supplied, answer any questions, and ask for the sale right away.

It is critical that you phrase your request correctly.

Asking a close-ended (yes or no) question (e.g., "Shall I send you the terms and conditions?") rather than a vague, open-ended one (e.g., "So, what do you think?") can help you complete more deals faster.

3. Respond to your prospect's concerns

When many decision-makers or stakeholders are involved, your customer may require more explanation or reassurance about the facts you've provided.

According to LinkedIn's State of Sales Report 2021, while 60% of sellers say they always put the buyer first, only 24% of buyers concur.

So, pay close attention, make intelligent responses in a timely manner, and, where needed, ask probing questions. These will include:

Encourage your prospect to expound on any issues that are bothering them.

Assist you in fast getting to the bottom of their hesitancy.

Allow you to collect information in order to adequately answer their problems.

For example, you could remark, "If I'm hearing you correctly, it sounds like you're concerned about X." "Did I get that right?" You can then proceed to dispel your prospect's specific concerns by emphasizing how and why your product is the best fit for their needs.

4. Be prepared to bargain

Sales negotiation is an important element of the closing process, even if you've done an excellent job qualifying your prospect.

Your customer may be concerned about:

Price or rival offerings

Purchase timing or product compatibility

Unwillingness to commit to change

If you tackle a new customer's worries correctly, there are nearly always ways to reframe their perspective. Understanding and practicing how to overcome sales objections should be part of your continuous sales closing training.

You should also know what concessions, such as multi-item price discounts or free delivery, you're willing (or authorized) to make when closing a transaction.

5. Employ the proper sales closing method.

Because various prospects demand different closing approaches, you may need to adjust your sales strategy from time to time. Here are a few examples of successful sales closing strategies.

If your prospect displays price worries, consider reducing specific product features or offering a value add-on such as free shipping.

If your prospect is hesitant to make a change, give them the opportunity to trial your product for free for a limited time.

If your customer is unsure about the product fit, give them a particular example of what they stand to benefit (for example, "By signing this contract today, you'll have reduced your administrative costs by X% this time next quarter").

Remember to ask for the sale again at this point. Use a simple query like, "I can offer a special, reduced subscription term of six months." "Can you commit to this plan right now?"

6. Follow up with your leads

If, despite your best efforts, the prospect requests additional time to examine your offer, you must determine the appropriate moment to follow up.

A decent rule of thumb is to send a sales follow-up email or phone call after one or two days for single buyers and four to five days for buying groups (to allow time for them to discuss the purchase choice).

When you do reach out, make sure to recap the highlights of your sales offering and remind the prospect how your product or service would benefit them.

7. Know when to let go.

If your prospect is still unwilling to sign on the dotted line, try to resurrect the contract by:

I'm contacting them to see if they have any other questions.

Inquiring about their preferred next step

Inquire personally if they are still interested in doing business with you.

When you've determined that the deal isn't going to complete, move it to your cold files and record the experience in your CRM so you can apply what you've learned (and potentially reestablish contact) in the future.

"Remain focused, persevere in your outreach efforts, and drive value for buyers in your sales conversations, and you'll soon see an increase in sales wins."

CHAPTER 7

Using Technology in Sales

Today's business is all about harnessing technology to make even the most mundane tasks faster and more successful, and sales is no exception. Although sales is still primarily a person-to-person transaction, using specific tools or software can assist make the sales process more efficient and personal for the sales team and potential consumers than prior techniques.

1. Use Analytics Tools for a Metrics-Based Approach Analytics tools (for example, Google Analytics) should be at the heart of every modern, dynamic sales process. Metrics derived from interactions with your content enable you to make informed judgments when fine-tuning your sales procedures. The metrics-driven approach to growing your sales pipeline will gradually broaden your qualified leads funnel, resulting in more sales.

2. Employ a Customer Relationship Management System

A strong CRM with drip email and text messaging software that allows you to arrange leads into qualified versus unqualified types is one method to use technology into sales. The automated follow-up system assists your sales team in following up with people, and the organization informs them of who and when to contact. To maintain your company's name in front of people, automated drip messages should be sent out on a regular basis.

3. Make use of a Price Quote Generator

Automating bespoke price quotes is a terrific approach to capture interest and lead data from prospective buyers online. A price quote generator can provide dynamic pricing that is tailored to each customer's specific requirements. The final pricing is email-gated and sent directly to clients as a lead magnet, ensuring that their first website visit will not be their last.

4. Configure Automated Text Messages and Canned Responses

When people don't want to buy, they usually have the same objections: they need to think about it, they don't have the money, they weren't expecting to pay so much, they need someone's permission to proceed, or they want a guarantee. To address these arguments, use automated SMS messages or prefabricated responses with YouTube videos.

5. Use a Content Experience Platform to Personalize Content

A content experience platform (CEP) is one piece of technology that you can use. This tool will assist you in personalizing material for each consumer, whether they are new to your business or have been on your email list for some time. A CEP organizes your content and provides relevant stuff to boost audience engagement. You'll streamline your sales process while also increasing revenue.

Make a Lead Scoring System.

Creating a lead scoring system, which is a technique to quantify the possibility of an opportunity, is one way firms may use technology to assist enhance their sales operations. It also assists businesses in making better judgments about when and how to pursue leads. Leads are assessed based on their potential of converting into consumers, allowing organizations to prioritize the most promising leads.

7. Configure Chatbots to Respond to Questions

Chatbots are an effective and very simple approach to use technology to improve your sales process. I recommend using these helpful tools to assist consumers with typical queries or issues. For example, if someone inquires about whether one of your products has a specific feature, your chatbot can direct them to the appropriate model and answer frequently asked questions.

8. Gather More Information

Data is all around you; all you have to do is collect, collate, and analyze it before putting it to use. Increased sales should be right around the corner if you do so properly.

9. Use Social Media to Add Value

Social media allows you to build relationships with clients while learning about their behaviors and wants. Creating valuable yet engaging content warms up your prospects to your brand, allowing you to reach out to them as warm leads. You can cultivate relationships with thousands or millions of prospects, which will lead to increased sales.

10. Make Your To-Do List Automated

Businesses can improve their sales processes by utilizing automation, which automates repetitive procedures and chores on your to-do list, allowing you to focus on larger, more significant projects.

11. Create a Blog Content Database

Building a solid database of blog content on a company's website is one approach for them to incorporate more technology into their sales procedures. For starters, this is an excellent technique to boost the SEO of the website. The far greater value, however, is that it delivers a treasure mine of sales tools for each stage of the buyer's journey, from "problem" discovery to picking which brand to purchase from.

Pitch using Video and AI

Emails are not as engaging as video. You may now target consumer segments with video presentations and sales sequences thanks to new technologies. After testing the efficiency of your copy and script with AI tools, record video messages. Even if you don't get more leads, you may still create your own brand awareness as a sales representative.

CHAPTER 8

Effective Follow-Up

Sales experts understand that there is more to effective sales than simply waiting for new consumers to walk in or old customers to return on their own.

When attempting to convert either prospective or existing consumers, having an effective follow-up approach is critical.

Your sales follow-up goals can be divided into three basic groups.

First, consider the prospects. In other words, any potential clients whose needs correspond with those of your goods.

Cold calling potential consumers is a well-known outbound prospecting tactic, but it rarely yields results the first time.

Then there are your leads. These are potential clients who are interacting with you but have not yet purchased from you.

Finally, don't forget about your current consumers. Anyone who has previously purchased from you is worth a sales follow-up

This form of sales follow-up can be accomplished in a variety of ways. Traditionally, this can entail calling clients to drum up interest in new sales.

In today's business world, some decision makers use voicemail to filter their calls, so you might not have a chance to speak with them directly if you haven't paved the road beforehand.

To create trust in the connection, it's generally a good idea to use alternate possibilities as well.

If done correctly, follow-up emails or even text messages can be just as powerful as follow-up calls.

You might also use social media to reach out to potential customers. A well-placed LinkedIn private message can occasionally offer your sales process a significant boost.

Of course, you don't want to be so obsessed with follow-up that you irritate the consumer. That would be ineffective.

However, the majority of salespeople lose up far too quickly.

The value of follow-up in sales cannot be overstated.

According to Xant's Sales Development Survey 2021 study, five or less follow-up attempts are made in response to inbound sales leads by sales professionals.

The data reveals that initiating seven or more contact efforts results in 15% more relationships, therefore most should have persisted.

So, let's take a closer look at the advantages of including a sales follow-up procedure into your sales and marketing plan.

Benefits of Sales Follow-up

Effective follow-ups can rekindle the sales process and get it moving.

The three key benefits are greater client connections, a higher conversion rate, and increased customer retention.

1. Improved customer interactions

Making a connection with your customers is an important element of selling successfully. In the end, consumers buy from people, not corporations.

You'll be halfway there if you can build a decent grasp of your customer's demands and problem spots.

Following up on sales leads helps to create trust.

It demonstrates to potential clients that you are prepared to invest time in learning their concerns. You're demonstrating that you appreciate their business and are making an effort to build a relationship with them.

This will set you apart in a crowded market. That's how you cultivate the kind of brand loyalty that lasts.

2. Increased likelihood of finalizing a sale

It makes no difference whether you contact out to describe your sales proposition via follow-up calls, follow-up emails, text messages, or social media: It's the fact that you're following up in the first place.

The relationship is the most important thing. Not all prospective consumers are ready to buy when you first contact them.

That's OK. Because once they're in the market for a new product like yours, the fact that you've kept in touch on a regular basis will be important.

Your name will be at the top of their minds, and they will be more likely to contact you than your competitors.

So, if you give up after just a few sales calls, you could be missing out on a big number of successful sales leads.

3. Customer retention

Sometimes sales professionals regard customer retention as less important than acquiring new ones.

While new business is always good, typical sales training does not usually emphasize the fact that customer retention is far less expensive for firms than customer acquisition.

Customer retention, on the other hand, requires effort.

Unsatisfied customers are more likely to go to a competitor than to complain directly to you.

If this happens frequently, it will have an impact on your bottom line.

Worse, if you don't contact existing consumers, you'll never find out why this is happening, and you won't be able to remedy the problem.

If your sales team contacts existing clients on a regular basis as part of your follow-up strategy, those consumers are more likely to tell you why they're dissatisfied.

That means you'll be able to deal with the issue and perhaps keep them on board.

CHAPTER 9

Dealing with Challenges

If you run into a marketing challenge and cannot address it, you could see yourself wasting money or losing customers or leads.

To help your business be more successful, you have to figure out how to target the right audiences, reach them with the right content, and convert them to people who support your brand.

We've put together a list of the top 12 marketing challenges you're likely to run into and the solutions that can help.

1. Getting new customers for your business

Getting new customers is the entire purpose of your marketing campaign; you want people to find you, and you want them to buy your products or use your services.

If you're not getting new customers with your current campaign, it could be time for an overhaul. Take a look at your campaign and think about how you're targeting your audience. Are you trying to target an audience that is just too large?

Dial it back and target your local audience. Is the campaign's imagery not lining up with the demographic? Try a new design to see if it gets a better response.

2. Training your marketing team to get the best ROI

Training your marketing team is an ongoing effort. What worked in the marketing world a decade ago may not be what works for you today, for example, so you do need to focus on **researching current markets** and the tactics that work to reach your audiences.

Understand the skills each of your employees has and then decide if you need to outsource any of your marketing work. You may be surprised at where there are **skill gaps that still need to be filled.**

Or, you can **hire highly-specialized freelance marketing professionals** to get the job done. Connect with over 15,000 strategists, writers and designers today in

3. Keeping up with the last global changes

Keeping up with global changes is another marketing challenge that many businesses run into. As the globe becomes ever more connected, people are getting influenced by content from all over the planet.

Keeping up with those influences isn't simple. If engagement differs across markets, **then you need to think about why some countries are recognizing your brand more easily than others.**

The solution for this issue is to focus on getting to know your audiences, targeting the right audiences, and making sure you have content that follows, at least in some ways, current trends.

4. Expanding your brand into other countries

Expanding your brand in another country isn't just about offering it there. You also need to think about how to promote it, get to know your local audiences, and be sure you're keeping up with the competition.

To help yourself, define your target audience. Then, **consider taking action to resolve language barriers.** Using content creators to help with promotion could be supportive of your efforts, too, since they know the local lingo.

5. Budgeting for your marketing campaigns

It can be expensive to market to more than just your local community. It also gets expensive when you start expanding into different marketing modalities, such as going to live ads or marketing across multiple social media channels.

Budgeting issues can be resolved by **staying focused on your campaign.** Start small and go slow to see which campaigns get the most interaction.

Then, double down on those options. You should see a better return on investment by doing this, which can help you reduce budget issues caused by trying to reach too many people too quickly.

6. Struggling with a lack of resources

Not every business is going to start with the same resources to cover all the markets you want to reach. Even if you have enough budget, you may not have the staff needed to carry out your campaign to its fullest potential.

The solution? Expand slowly, and outsource anything you can't do in-house. **That might mean outsourcing your content**, for example, so you can focus on other aspects of your business.

7. Database management: Keeping your data accessible

Your database is going to grow larger over time as you gather more information. You need to keep it organized, so you can access the information you need when you need it and see if you are getting a good **return on your investments (ROI).**

Using a unified marketing and analytics platform will keep you organized. If you take this database on the cloud, you'll be able to access it from anywhere where you have internet access, making it easier to do your job in or outside the office.

You may also want to look for automation software and artificial intelligence that can **automatically sort data** and send you reports.

8. Handling market changes as they arise

The market is constantly changing. A competitor could go out of business, or the wants and needs of your customers may shift.

Studying **market trends** can help you stay apprised of changes and help you adapt quickly as they occur.

9. Standing out from the crowd

Another serious marketing challenge that people run into today is the problem of too much choice. **Customers can become overwhelmed when there are too many choices out there,** and having so many options on the market can cause disruptions in sales and services rendered.

The same is true of marketing strategies. **You have many options to reach customers,** but it can get overwhelming to try to reach everyone through every marketing technique.

Stick with just two or three marketing tools to start with, because sometimes you can do more with less.

10. Increased

Of course, the fact that markets are now global means that you have increased competition in your niche no matter what it is. There are not only the old markets you used to use but also new markets that are starting to develop.

As you build your marketing campaign, think carefully about where you want to be seen. Starting locally may help you get a **stronger foundation for your company**, and then you can expand out as you become profitable and well-known enough to compete with competitors.

CHAPTER 10

Continuous Growth

However, many organizations do not apply the principle of continuous improvement to their digital marketing. This astounds us. Not only because the phrase "a website is never finished" has been used for decades, but we've also experienced firsthand the great outcomes that can be accomplished by constantly learning and making

improvements.
As a result, the goal of this essay is to clarify common misconceptions regarding continuous improvement and demonstrate how it can be applied in digital marketing to give a competitive advantage and assist corporate growth.
How can continuous improvement help your business?
The advantages of utilizing continual improvement in your digital marketing are obvious. So, here are a few of the top reasons to use it into your marketing strategy to benefit your company.
Increased income and ROI as your marketing approach becomes more effective as a result of incremental strategic and tactical changes
Increased efficiency since you can develop your digital marketing utilizing real-time user data to guarantee you're focusing on the most effective plans and techniques to satisfy the needs of your target clients.

Reduced expenses and risk since you may stretch your marketing investment over time and constantly learn to devote budget and time to the most impactful locations.

Create more lasting and mutually beneficial relationships with your audience by changing to better connect and engage them.

All aspects of your digital marketing can benefit from continuous enhancement. We've included some suggestions for incorporating continuous improvement into some of the most popular channels and methods to help you maximize them even more.

Strategy.

Monitoring macro and micro data affecting your organization is critical because it allows you to determine whether strategic alterations are required to adapt to capitalize on opportunities or avoid dangers. You can A/B test your tactical mix to confirm that it is effective, and then alter according on the results. A clear and simple monthly, weekly, or daily report is required to provide clarity on your strategy impact, depending on your type of business. For this, we recommend Google Data Studio, and you can learn more about how to improve your reporting in our previous article.

Website is one of the platforms that many firms develop and then abandon, with 42% of marketers only making significant changes to their website once or fewer per year (HubSpot survey). This is a significant missed opportunity because you could be improving the user experience, feature enhancements, performance enhancements, particularly around your Core Web Vitals scores, conversion rate optimization, and content gaps, to mention a few. Granite 5 employs a Growth-Driven Design technique to structure the website improvement process.

In a recent article, 5 critical areas you should be checking in your regular website health check, we go into additional methods you can continuously monitor and enhance your

website performance.

Email This channel may easily be enhanced on a regular basis by doing A/B tests on elements in your emails such as with and without photos, different headlines, modified design, plain text vs HTML, different types of CTAs, and varying mailing days and hours. All current email marketing software will provide you with data from these experiments, allowing you to constantly improve and satisfy your customers.

Automation Many organizations who utilize automation in their marketing through CRM and marketing platforms like HubSpot tend to construct and then forget about them, assuming they are performing their job. Regardless of how good your automation system is, you should always search for ways to improve it. Is the content being consumed by the recipients? Is it possible to develop additional automated workflows to boost efficiency and deliver a better customer experience?

Brand administration

You may believe that once you've identified your brand, this will be a static area. However, as any great marketer will tell you, obtaining brand recognition among your target clients at the point of purchase and retaining that top-of-mind brand position is critical and demands ongoing effort. Your brand should evolve in response to market developments and your strategic focus, while remaining faithful to your fundamental brand principles. See this amazing example of a little-known brand called Apple doing exactly that.

Social networking sites

Social media networks now provide a wealth of data that can help you determine whether your activity is productive. You can compare this to your company's key performance indicators (KPIs) to see if you're on track. By analyzing this data, you will be able to understand how you need to adjust your content, posting times, type of content, messaging, and even the platform's performance in order to continuously enhance your social strategy and better fulfill your business goals and customer demands.

Content promotion

Once content, particularly website content, has been published, it's all too simple to let it sit on your site, presuming it's driving traffic and assisting conversions. However, analyzing your content for relevance, engagement, and purpose on a frequent basis is an important aspect of content continual development. All content will fall into one of four categories, and you should tailor it accordingly:

Maintain - If the content is serving its function and generating results, it should keep its **position.**

Optimize - If the content is not performing as expected, it must be optimized. Is it using the appropriate keywords? Is there a reason for it? Are you responding to your customers' inquiries?

Rewrite - If the content is older or the topic has changed, it should be updated to incorporate more current and engaging content in order to better serve your audience.

Retire - If the content no longer serves a function, is no longer relevant to your audience, and isn't delivering any SEO advantage, it should be retired.

Advertising.

The beauty of digital advertising is the speed with which modifications can be made to ads, as well as the transparency of the performance of those ads in relation to your goals. To get the most out of your digital advertising, whether it's Google PPC, LinkedIn sponsored content, or Instagram shopping ads, you should analyze its success on a regular basis and make gradual changes based on the data. This also allows you to supplement earned and owned media with bought media to maximize on-market chances.

Conclusion

"As we conclude this journey toward realizing your sales potential, keep in mind that success in sales is about more than just techniques; it is also about a mindset of continuous improvement." Accept rejection as a stepping stone to success, and see objections as chances for understanding and connection. Continue to improve your communication abilities, gain a better understanding of your audience, and establish trust. Always try to provide value and solutions. With hard work and the knowledge obtained from this book, you'll be on your way to a future of skyrocketing sales and infinite potential. Now go out there and make your mark in the sales industry!"